Philip Becker Goetz

Kallirrhoe

A Dramatic Poem

Philip Becker Goetz

Kallirrhoe
A Dramatic Poem

ISBN/EAN: 9783337337445

Printed in Europe, USA, Canada, Australia, Japan

Cover: Foto ©Thomas Meinert / pixelio.de

More available books at **www.hansebooks.com**

Kallirrhoe

A
Dramatic
Poem

By
Philip Becker Goetz

Buffalo ❧ The Peter Paul
Book Company ❧ 1896 ❧

Characters

KORESOS, a priest of Dionusos.

EURUPULOS, heir to the throne of Kaludon and brother to KALLIRRHOE.

CHOROS of priests.

KALLIRRHOE, beloved of Koresos.

AGLAIA, attendant to KALLIRRHOE, and beloved of EURUPULOS.

MESSENGER from the temple.

Attendants.

SCENE: KALUDON.

Time: The Regency of MELANIOS.

Kallirrhoe

KORESOS

O Dionusos, here before thine altar
After no ceaseless vigil of vain prayer
But scarce with wrath of lips grown cold ere thou
Didst hear my cry, I stand with offering
Stainless and pure and holy hands of thanks.
Thy pestilence hath spread from wall to wall,
Swept men and mothers, virgins and the bud
Of strength to everlasting shade beyond
The voice of love, whose unavailing eyes
Yearn from the loveless earth toward drearer Hades.
Still how her proud eyes keep their sullen level!
Who heard her sigh when her loved sire lay low
In death? While yet above his treasured urn
She sorrowed, came not one to whisper woe
And said her mother, too, decaying craved
Becoming burial? The head of her
Must wear this curse of partings populous!
For thou herein hast honored me thy priest,
Since at my supplication when she spurned
Me most and held her arrogance bolt-bright
Above my fettered soul, my rage outbrake
My bonds and there I vowed my remnant life
That she should feel the flame wherewith she blasted
My hope, my fair desire, and all sweet joy
Among staid precincts of mine adoration.

Here, then, Luaios, be thou paid: this stain
Of slaughtered goats with sacred ivy crowned
And dearer tendrils of the sunny vine;—
(Yet grant me strength to look beyond her eyes)—
Thus have I done; but thou, attendant, speak
Upon the advent of Kallirrhoe.

(Exit KORESOS.)

Enter CHOROS

Strophe A

Hence we passed with step of pain:
  For the rude voice of the pest,
    Moanings of dying,
    Oaths of defying,
    Sobs and low sighing
  Gave no rest.
Through the long nights thick with rain,
    The sacred wind,
    The brass bright-twined
Leafy beckoned in behest.

Strophe B

To the forest we came:
  "Dim Dodona, give us peace;
    Hear us, Zeus, oh grant us grace."
    Looked we then upon each face
  Of the warders of release,
Grim-eyed stare of each dame,—
    Their silvered hair
    By the silver moon

Seemed graceless, bare
Of our anxious boon.

Strophe C

"Blood the angered god demands.
The princeliest fair that head:
Else equal the life ye shed.
Lead the victim to his hands
Whom to avenge in holywise
Guilty the guiltless dies.
Speak no word but bind with bands
Brow of the sacrifice."

Antistrophe A

Hither came we in dismay
With more death to death of grief.
"Give us his blessing!"
Round us pale pressing
Cried they confessing
Hope's belief.
Silently we went our way
To greet our priest,
Ere they had ceased
Questioning the fatal leaf.

Antistrophe B

Him we found low-bowed.
"Hath Dodona given peace,
Heard our prayer and granted grace?"
Yet we guarded speech a space,
Fearing woe in heaven's release.

Taught, his eyes gathered cloud :
He raised his hands
And cried " 'Tis she
The god demands—
Kallirrhoe ! "

Antistrophe C

Now the dawn hath brought a morn
Most happy or most accursed,—
In ocean of woe immersed
Came and paceth toward its bourn
Tear-sad, if she can find
None of such kindly mind
Choosing death that she may scorn
Blast of the baleful wind.

Enter EURUPULOS

Hail, friend !   Tell me, is Koresos within ?

CHOROS

Truly thy haste of word imports strange news.

EURUPULOS

News that were better old to please that priest.

CHOROS

Thy lightness is unworthy thee and him
And thus of Dionusos whom he serves.

EURUPULOS

A fit phrase hast thou found herein for him !

CHOROS

What phrase? Speak, youth! What meanest thou in this?

EURUPULOS

What meaning lieth here I treasure close
For Koresos, not for his doting slaves!

CHOROS

Slaves? Doting slaves? Now be thou ware, and heed,
O youth, lest the high princely stock whence thou
Hast sprung, be laid in lowliness and shame
By this unseemliness,—strange blasphemy
That green years may insult the fruit of age,
Conservers of the past not promisers
Of laden ripeness from most dubious bud.
But the soft fall of sacred foot I hear.

KORESOS

What loud impatience of untutored years
Begins this fatal morn unhallowed strife?

CHOROS

Behold the prince, ill master of his tongue.

EURUPULOS

Had I been more a master I had left
Thee less a maker of such calm discourse;
But now my words were weak before my cause
And, to just Koresos I turn my thought
Engaging reminiscence of the woe
Which spreads this day destruction on my life.

KORESOS

Thou art most merciful: a noble race
Bespeaks this resolution to depose
Thy blood for thy rude-fated sister: I
Commend thy strength and dedicate thy love
For her among the gifts by far most grateful
To Dionusos.

EURUPULOS

           Speed of lofty wish
Aye marks the priest anticipating fact.
Surely to me her life is dear: more dear
Forsooth, than now to him who whispered menace
No longer since than in the month of flowers
When to her bosom alien to his vows
He hissed untimely end. Methinks his name
Is not unknown to thee, O Koresos.

KORESOS

Eurupulos, ask me no idle question.

CHOROS

Heed him, Eurupulos, I pray thee, heed!
Lest fate befall more keen than angry threat.

EURUPULOS

Here, then, before you both I bare my heart.
Know thou, O Koresos, that thou hast proved
Thyself a practiced archer in the doles
Of death: for I, a prince, before thy servants
Humble myself to shame thee what thou art.

Tears now avail me not, for she most dear
Of all my kin, my sister, searching long
Hath found a life to answer for her own
Demanded, as thou sayst, by Dionusos.
And her she found is of all women crowned
The utmost wonder of our realm's extent,
The high, fierce fire my heart supports and feeds
With proudest blood: and when I might attain,
Starts this decree, a cloud across my hope.
How have they sinned, my sister or her mate?
Tell me, just Koresos, and I will pause.
More still than fate, more ruthless, too, thou standest!
Hear me disclose thee to thyself, a dread
And fearful curse to thy most holy office
And yet more awful to this land of thine!

CHOROS

Stay, youth, thy rage: see how his hate he lowers!

KORESOS

Wilt thou declare this fevered love, yet live?
No oracle forbids the sacrifice
Of thee for thy loved sister or that wonder
Of thy dominion.   Lift thy heart to deeds
And be not thou content, O puissant prince,
To bruit devotion in the ears of men,
And, when thou mightst earn endless honor, fail.

CHOROS

O youth, reflect upon his words, and win.

EURUPULOS

Thou knowest well my duty's debt to men.
Exalted in the hearts of Kaludon
My father held his throne and not a breath
Of abject rumor ever soiled his rule.
Thumenides is dead and with him died
My queenly mother.   I am left, sole remnant—
After Melanios, our childless regent—
Of their torn fortune: were it right that I,
Sole son to stead my house, beget fair offspring,
And hold this power where it stood of yore,—
Should leave my line and issueless, unloved
Of gods or men, because I hear no voice
Of destiny, die for Dodona's cry?
Not that I love my life in what I am
But what I see unripened if I die,
Prevents the sacrifice for those I love.
Hear mine appeal, for yonder in the distance
Methinks they move, calmly and sadly dear.
Save them, almighty Koresos, oh save!

CHOROS

Strophe A

Heavy that joy in whose heart
Sorrow must pay for its life:
Who gave the one
Its light and sun?
And who cast the gloom
On the other's bloom?

Surely the gods were at strife
Thus to perplex man with art.

Strophe B

What is length of days, or strength, or praise ?
 They pass like the fragrance of flowers :
For a time we charm away alarm
 Yet bend to the merciless powers
 Of death, whose breath
Blasts as it sweeps with hurricane harm.

Antistrophe A

Tears fill her eyes as she nears
 Solemnly proud yet demure :
 Who knows her thought ?
 Why thus she sought
 Chill death and despair
 For a friend to bear ?
 Noble that friend and sure,
Tried and devoid of low fears !

Antistrophe B

Since she loved her life, what was her strife—
 The friend who in utter surrender
Robs herself of the light, of love's dear sight ?
 May Zeus and his mercy attend her,
 In peace release
Breath from the fairness she flings to the night.

(*Enter KALLIRRHOE and AGLAIA.*)

KORESOS

Hail! maiden, happy in thy faithful friends.

KALLIRRHOE

Little my joy when health allots heart-sickness.

EURUPULOS

O sister, knewst thou strength, sorrow were strange.

KALLIRRHOE

Thou, too, wouldst have me die unjustly, brother?

EURUPULOS

Far from my will such thought, Kallirrhoe;
Yet, sister, would this day had never dawned,
Ere thou and I and all we love in one
Swift stroke of common fate had left the light.

KORESOS

Hast thou, a brother, not before this hour
Revealed to her, thy sister, thy disease?

EURUPULOS

She knoweth all. For, tell me, Koresos,
What woman lovely in the eyes of men
Lifts clear brow and most innocent of ill
Knows not the spell she casts about the sense?
And equally no woman but divines
The kindred power in another's beauty.
Had I ne'er spoken (as no brother heart
Would grant), she would have read my secret passion,
Caught it and phrased it to my startled ears

And sent it speeding one hot eagerness
Through all my frame.   Trust thou a woman's guess.
Well knoweth she my love for fair Aglaia,—
Aglaia glad in me and ready so
To die for her, my sister and her mistress.
What though she be low-born and Agrios,
Her father kept the hillside flecked with flock
And pressed the oozy dugs and sent the curd
To princely tables?   What though thus ignobly
A toiler with hard hands he wrought long years?
As from dark earth blossoms the purest lily
And from the pool the lotus radiant,
So issued she—a glory of no pride.
Hers is the loveliness a god would woo;
High-dowered, beauteous, and rare with graces
Forgotten through the jealousy of fates,
Who give their gifts that men may worship them,
Not love too well the gifted lest the bale
Of smitten mind disturb the might of kings.
As, in the days of old, fair Leda's child
Waving her wayward tresses gold against
Golden Apollo, made distraught huge Theseus
Till tremblingly he caught her to his heart
And bore her off a curse upon the lips
Of unbelieving men, who, once beholding,
Smothered their oaths and prayed she gaze their way !
Then, be her stock obscure, yet gentleness
Never knew welcome in a breast more high.
What better proof of most exalted worth ?
She leaves her life to give another life.

CHOROS

Discretion marks his words who first in rudeness
Addressed our pious ears; and why in meekness
He here appeareth, know I not unless
The strife of gladly losing one he loveth
And sadly keeping thus another love
Hath tired a mad invention unto calm.
Nevertheless, foreboding fills my spirit
Lest in sweet words dark omen of swift fate
And keen disaster lurk, since silent stands
Absorbed and hesitant with lucent truth
Holiest Koresos. Speak, master, speak!

KORESOS

Before I speak, confirm me my conjecture:
Of thee with unuplifted eye I ask,
Aglaia, but one only word and answer
Me truly as thou art a woman born
Beauteous and perilous to mortal peace.
Art thou the child of lowly Agrios,
Herdsman and keeper of meek-moving sheep
In Kaludon, who, maimed in combat once
Among yon rugged mountains, limped in flight
To us, praying for aid?   This would I know.

AGLAIA

Thou hast conjectured truly: I am his.

CHOROS

Flashing his eyes with sign of godlike fury!
Nor can I aught discern of his intent.

KORESOS

Thou knewest, then, thou wast a slave born, bred,
And willing still to manifest thyself
No whit superior to thine origin!
Here stood Eurupulos a willing aid
To veil with pleadings dim the face of truth:
How deep and wide and high and universal
His love for thee! Here, too, Kallirrhoe
Stood like a stone, unheeding, deaf, the dread
And potent oracle of Zeus. Is't thus
Ye meant to baffle gods with treachery?
Are ye so ignorant as thus to deem
Bright godhead blind to human cheat and fraud?
In very truth however tortuous
The path of guiltiness, yet be ye ware
Upon the fleeing heel more subtly follow
The lidless fates with hiss of retribution
Armed strong, of speed unwearied, hot with hate.
A curse shall fall upon your unbent heads!
O Father Zeus, ere suppliant they sink
Upon their knees I pray thee pity them;
Forgive their deed, for life is sweet to youth
And uninstructed in the errant means
Of sin they wrought this insult to thy power!
Forgive them, Father Zeus, and hear my prayer.

(*Weeping, he sinks exhausted upon the earth.*)

CHOROS

He lies on the ground;
He utters no sound!

What shall we say?
Hither come, pray,
Oh gather ye round!

KALLIRRHOE

Now he revives and lifts again his head,
Will I be venturesome and solve my doubt.

AGLAIA

Prithee, not harshly on my poor behalf!
Or life or death, in equal grief henceforth
I live a slave in deed thus humbled low.

EURUPULOS

Oh speak not so, Aglaia. For, as night
Opposed to purple west rises from sea,
So sorrow comes from gladness, lighting so
A thousand stars else ever undescried!

KALLIRRHOE

Brother, lead her away that I may seek
The priest, who glances as with urgent threat.

                     (*Exeunt EURUPULOS and AGLAIA.*)

KORESOS

Whither away? Not yet upon your knees?

KALLIRRHOE

Distress thee not that thus they wander forth;
Since ignorance of wrong is right's first shield.

KORESOS

Thy last word suiteth well a weak defense.

KALLIRRHOE

No woman needs a man to hint her weak
When her strong master stoops to such a phrase.

KORESOS

Enough of words: the day would end ere thou
Hadst satisfied thy most untoward tongue.

KALLIRRHOE

Why, then, that gaze that bade me stay behind?

KORESOS

Kallirrhoe, thou hast as stubborn spirit
Untamed, unflexible by holy ways
As by the softer touch of human love.

KALLIRRHOE

Yet tell me, tutored guardian of the gods,
Why thou so fervently hast disallowed
Aglaia die for me? My tried Aglaia,
Alone of all my friends found faithful still!
What weary days I searched and vainly searched;
And at the last when none appeared in aid,
Came she with timid voice and tearful prayer
Placing her wan hands to my fevered head
And whispered as she kneeled beside me there—
We both quite silvered in the last moonlight
Mine eyes seemed destined to behold—there clung

And syllabled she meant to give herself
For me.   How I rejoiced in this great gift
Zeus sent in answer to my love of life !
Wherefore I joyed in her, wherefore in life,
None save all-seeing Zeus can ever know,—
Since dimness is the dawn of womanhood,
Wearing her mystery invisibly
A crown secure against who dares aspire.
Now have I done.   Think not I bend: I stand
A rock against the waves of circumstance,
Asking their hungry violence no peace.
Yet ere I go, again I pray thee tell
How that Aglaia may not die for me ?

KORESOS

Thou knowest but too well the fatal fault.

KALLIRRHOE

Fatal at least : but fault I cannot grant.

KORESOS

Both : since it counsels thee prepare thyself
To die and charges insolence to Zeus.

KALLIRRHOE

How?   Insolence !   Wherein so grave a charge?

KORESOS

In that the oracle demanded clearly
That who should die vicarious for thee
Must be thy peer.

KALLIRRHOE
Is not, then, this fulfilled?

KORESOS
A slave for thee, a maid of royal blood?

KALLIRRHOE
And wherefore not?   O Koresos, declare.

KORESOS
When dogs are steeds; owls, doves; earth, air; sea, sky;
Then may a slave to lowest of the free
Be peer: e'en then remote from him in worth.

KALLIRRHOE
O Koresos, a life for life is just.

KORESOS
No priest dares offer victims with one blot!

KALLIRRHOE
Blot may be whiteness to the eyes of gods!

KORESOS
Think not they lean with such a patient eye:
With chill austerity severe they rule.
Such insult to the god we would appease,
Would stir a greater plague than Kaludon
Hath yet endured.   Speak, then, no idle word.

KALLIRRHOE

Then, Koresos, look thou upon me well.
This is the sacrifice thy hidden thought
Demands.   If I dared loose my tongue this hour
In utterance, I could enlighten all.
See that thou keen the sacrificial blade
Till I bring me enrobed and filled with all
True bravery of soul that I may die,
Though I be woman, with no tear save red.
That me thou wouldst sublime in peerless death,
Allowing none may die that I may live,
Not flatters me: a barren, foolish truth!

KORESOS

And wherefore foolish if a truth?

KALLIRRHOE

                    Device
Of their own gain makes wise the meanest fools.

KORESOS

Dark are thy words.

KALLIRRHOE

                    That I spake lucent terror!
The hand of man, not Zeus, created slaves.
Cold kings and priests august, the strong of earth
Must find a mode to save their hands from stain,
Writing a deeper on their sordid hearts.

KORESOS

Wouldst thou so think, were not thy life at stake?

KALLIRRHOE

Would I were cruel,—so to answer thee;
But I beseech thee ere I deck myself
In ritual of plague-atoning death
The last time for the roving eyes of who
Will come in witness of a rude deceit,
Confirm me of sincerity and ruth
In this thy reading of the oracle.

KORESOS

One moment ere the sacrificial knife
Reaves thee of life, I shall declare: nor else.

KALLIRRHOE

I go.

KORESOS (*as she moves away*)

How my soul follows in her way!
Scarce can I stay my voice from utterance
Of her blest name. "Kallirrhoe!" I fain
Would call, to bid her yet retrace her step. . .
Now Zeus be praised for hate! From my soul's deep
I hate her, seeing she hath made me love!

CHOROS

Strophe A

Full of sorrow and of cares
Weary he passed;

On his brow no crown he wears
Though a king of men he be,
Heavy-hearted as the sea,
    Leaving at last
Mirth and joy of earth, soul free.

Strophe B

And darknesss lieth beyond the breath
Last drawn as hence man hasteneth.
    Who hath pierced the gloom of the tomb?
    Who hath brought relief to low grief?
As leaves in autumn fall dead
And parent tree overhead
Knoweth them nevermore,
Like unto autumn's store,
    Fruit and the garlands of spring,
We fade away, in a moment decay,
    Tainted, a filthy thing!

Strophe C

Shall we sorrow and, sorrowing, double woe
Or be glad and in gladness lightly go
Over wastes of despair where she spreads her snare
    Woven of thought and of care?

Antistrophe A

Why a godhead, if no aid
    Answer worn knees?
Hide the brow in ivy shade,
Droop the eye with vinous drowse,
Clang the cymbals in carouse

Doubly with glees,—
Iakchos' jocund raid!

Antistrophe B

The gods in bidding mankind endure
Allow no bane but hides a cure.
Ariadne cried to the tide
As her Theseus dead to her fled:
The swept wave, deaf to appeal,
Responded naught as the keel
Arrogant spurned vain Crete.
Turned, she saw at her feet,
Tall in no glory of earth,
Brighter than star with white Artemis far,
Dread Dionusos in mirth!

Antistrophe C

He requited with love her questioning grief,
To a woman bereft a god gave relief:
Shall a priest be abandoned who dedicates
Life and on godhead waits?

Epodos

Where lies, O Eros, thy kindliness?
Thus to destroy a priest,
Thus to mock the just, to consume the true
By deep-sown fire of a human eye!
Blaspheme I never, rather bless
Thy potent will and deity,
Yet on my master at least
Thou hast brought the dubious gift of rue.

(*Enter KORESOS slowly.*)

CHOROS

What thoughts are thine, O Koresos, our lord,
That ever with the earth thou hast discourse
And never upward to the air art won?

KORESOS

'Tis that I question earth to answer me,
And finding still reply unwritten where
I seek, yet gaze on emptiness as dreaming.

CHOROS

Surely the load upon thine age is grown
Too grave to wear; youth were a fitter time.

KORESOS

Thou speakest, then, of her whom young in years
I loved, still love, and shall not cease to love?

CHOROS

Strange that thy wisdom and ripe mastery
Of humors kin to vigorous prime submit
Their strength unto a scorning maiden.   Royal
I grant her with unsullied blood of sires
Endued and with the valid victories
Of perished generations beautiful;
Nathless, what gainest thou—advanced from bloom
Of youth, from springtime of man's passioning,
From the first fine delirium of vein,
From freshness and the thrilling zest of morn

(What morn clear youth awakes to manhood's mist)?
Canst thou without the tinct regret at folly
Hide blossom of thy plucking in her hair?
Or wage enfrenzied warfare widely sweet
Upon her cheek? Cling lip and interlock
Fond fingers? Think thou on this vainness, judge
Thyself if not most mad and ill-advised
Too late thy wooing show most indecorous.

KORESOS

Oh say not so! Too well I know her hate
That settled strong as destiny hath blasted
My hope and long desire of life and bliss.
Methinks the very temple-stones one day
In witness of my truth must far proclaim
Their knowledge of my knees bent low to Zeus
Remedial. But all is past: so pass
Much cherished dreams whence we awake to earth
From lands incredible beyond our ken.
Pity for her inhabiteth my heart,
Yet Dionusos spake and Dionusos
Shall be obeyed if no free-born present
The price: in death vicarious to die.
Aye, even as I speak, hither she moves.

(As *KALLIRRHOE* enters)

What means thy garb of cheer, Kallirrhoe,
Thy loosened hair, these arms outspread, this gait
As if the festal timbrel taught thy step
Obedience to its call? No festival
Is here, but sombre rite of formal death

On thee decreed, not lacking piety
Of yonder holy knife and my true hand
Swift to surrender thee unto our god,
Who to allay rough crest and ceaseless wave
Of loss demands the princely price of thee.

KALLIRRHOE

No ill-conjectured method in my robe,
O priest,—if still thou ponder and not once;
On failure, yield the answer aye unanswered.
And lest thou fail to read, mine enterprise
Be here to teach.   What! shall the victim wail
Against the god's decree interpreted
In mode of grace by comely deputy?
That were to rail on fate, blaspheme the just,
Assume the heifer's brute appeal from pain.
For here, devout, our master Koresos
Tells Kaludon to kill a princess, prize
At word, as asked by dying citizens;
New irony of power that subjects' cry
Demands and wins the fall of nobler state!
When died a god for man, to found such justice?
So am I come in all obedience,
Ripe for the happy god, one soul the more,
One grape starved Dionusos crunches thus
To burnish the sleek brow one red the more
And fling Persephone the corporal husk!
How! wilt thou charge me sacrilegious now,
Because I count most vain enervate incense,
And vain your shrieking beasts with taunt of wreath
Encircling their decorous innocence?

KORESOS

Cease, on thy life!

KALLIRRHOE

Thou shalt hear all.

KORESOS

Insult
Not Dionusos. Though thou spurn the man
Of me, bethink thee that on this my brow
The dreadful choice of priesthood sits enthroned,
The which thus rashly and in wrath to vex
Shall bring more horror than mere loss of breath!

KALLIRRHOE

Of all I have bethought me and—I speak.

KORESOS

Better were peace and good than sin and death.

KALLIRRHOE

A weak word, priest! For though I speak a sin
In tonguing here my hot soul, I am true.

KORESOS

Woe, woe! thy shroud is sin and taints thy white.

KALLIRRHOE

Then, as a king begat, queen bare me, I
Scorning degree, control, and niggard truth
Within the meditated phrase, entreat

Thee, Lord of all the world, O Zeus, be kind!
And if I sin, inspire a grand sin now!

KORESOS

Again before the god of Kaludon
In awful fear I warn thee, curb thy tongue!

CHOROS

He speaks intending favor; timely heed;
Allow I join entreaty for thy good.

KALLIRRHOE

Away! I reck not longer, but declare
My heart that, ere it burst to sanguine bloom
Upon the blade, pierces for utterance
My breast intact. By all the gods in heaven,
You never loved me, Koresos, but still
Within thyself held hate of me, designed
The overthrow of all our house, and scared
Eurupulos until he proved one night
Within the sacred grove his righteous arm
Upon thy crippled form!

KORESOS
'Tis false, I—

KALLIRRHOE
                    Nay,
Attend! I will not scant a syllable.
And then thou didst devise how that by love
And craft thou mightst deceive and vanquish him

By snaring me unto thine arms; but spurned
And loathed by me, acute to pierce and keen
To cut thy covetous conceits, recourse
Was thine to Dionusos and Dodona.
Nay, hear me home! Thou hast my latest word.
What heed the gods the hand, so up to them
Twine sweet submissive scent and savors thick?
But thee I know from thy shrunk foot's weak print
E'en to the chill of thy foul-scheming heart,—
A plausive priest, a most corrupt impostor!

KORESOS

Now may the gods—but seize her, bind her arms!
And may—

KALLIRRHOE

Thy curse upon thine own life fall,
And mayst thou live among men tedious days,
Ceaseless increasing thine infirmities
From hour to hour until thy sorrows bow
Thee down a living corse close to the earth
To make thee show a cringer to the ground
As now to gods and men. And when the end
Befalls, with blasted eyeballs, impotent
And fain to speak thy woe, with palsied tongue
And still more withered shape than this thy case,
Alone, unloved of men, a sport of gods
Then ware of thee, reviled and outcast mayst
Thou die in misery, unburied lie
In wildered waste of earth where human hand

May never strew a pious dust-grain o'er
Thy wretched flesh.   May rapine birds too vile,
Too sick for honest carrion, draw near
And pick thee piece from rotting piece that there
Quite peered in wretchedness with merit here,
Though formless, spared in not one ache the less,
But in each several rifled part of thee
A realm of woe, endlessly mayst thou shriek
In ghastly music through the dawnless night,
Haunting the hollow spaces of the air,
Hearing no answer but reverberate pain
Leaping thy scattered lips remote from Zeus!

CHOROS

He swoons! attendants, ho! . . . . Lead her within.
                              (*Exeunt all save CHOROS.*)

CHOROS

Strophe A

Wherever upon the ways of the earth
   Man moves, he moves not alone:
      But attendant, invisible, two
Hover: one is woe and the other is mirth;
      One smarting a smile with rue
   And one to cheer every moan.
And which, when they battle, shall win or lose,
Seems never a man's to choose,
No more than to bid the sun arise
Or hang the thick clouds from the skies.

Strophe B

Many degrees of sight Zeus gave
  And he taught us to gaze and be glad;
    He laughs with our joy and is calm at our grief;
    He looks with no pity and sends no relief
  For he heaps with distresses the sad,
Sinners of choice whom no prayers can save
        When they read awry.
        E'en to kings and high
        Of the world when they cry
          He deafens his ear,
            Placid with power, unmoved as a flower
          His face regarding man's fear.

Strophe C

  For he taught us the right,
    Not his the blame
      If the better eye miss and betray:
    The king sees wide and discovers the same
  With a god's wing-traveling sight;
        And the slave is least,
        For he toils, is a beast—
      For defect to the gods, and to man for play.

Antistrophe A

  If, then, the strictest of eyes, and of ears
    The finest leaned to the prayer
      And in justice noted and made
  Answer, Koresos may be heedless of fears
      And slay with a cheerful blade,

Nor quake as, oozing through hair,
The rich life gives the ransoming seal:
Since, one destroyed shall a thousand heal.
The next grey dawn are no mourners seen:
Fair Kaludon awakes and is clean.

Antistrophe B

Lofty however a mortal be
  And a boast to the land of his race,
    The gods but command him, no mercy is theirs;
    Their-faces are alien, devoid of cares,
  Their spirits unclouded. What grace
Owe they to us? They would never decree
      Even to their own
      Sons of earth, sky-sown,
      Incorruptive bone,
        Eye proof against night,
          Sinews of steel that can mock the deal
        Of discovering dart in the fight.

Antistrophe C

Dionusos brought low
  With swift disease;
    And almighty Zeus to the loud despair
  Sent peace in pall to bid from these
No more than Kallirrhoe go:
      More solicitous
      Or more just to us
      There was never god o'er the vaulted air.

Enter EURUPULOS

Tell me, O men, delay me not, with speed
Resolve me—Koresos—is he within?

CHOROS

Not doubtfully thy question bears its answer;
But, in thy turn, say wherefore pallid cheek,
Breath-interrupted phrases, hurried eyes?

EURUPULOS

I fain would learn the deed, whether performed
Or haply unaccomplished yet and waiting.
If I might enter—

CHOROS

No impiety!
By Dionusos, who would stay the knife,
May he ignobly perish.   Hold, no further
Advance lest thunder and insanity
Strike palsy through thine every vein and harrow
And shrivel thy man's vigor into naught.

EURUPULOS

Hark ye! so many marvels throng to loose
Themselves articulate, yet credible
To none, I needs must pause which to propose.
Briefly, Melanios the King hath passed
To me the scepter.

CHOROS

How?   What favor hast
Thou found, to be preferred before his end?

EURUPULOS

He is no more.

CHOROS

What means this word?   Oh speak!

EURUPULOS

Shall I repeat?   He is no more.   He breathes
Never again the breath of life, but now
Awaits the journey ever at the ebb
Until due rites be paid.

CHOROS

Oh heavy news!
The manner of his end?

EURUPULOS

I would relate
Were I but more immediate to aid
Kallirrhoe.   I cannot speak and think
She dies an arm-stretch whence I stand.

CHOROS

Defer
Thy cares to fate; how meetly may the earth
Be ordered, 'tis divine solicitude.

EURUPULOS

Know, then, as I returned Aglaia hence,
To me swift-footing o'er the mead there posted
A messenger who urged a further speed,
How that the king grew wan with fading breath.
Alarmed, I hastened where he sat amid
Ignorant and too willing ministrants.
For one would soothe his brow, another loose
His robe, and still another cried him air,
Until I came and swept them with my hand
Away and backward from his struggling breast.
He seemed to sink beneath a load on's heart,
At every effort weaker coping, while,
Dumb and imploring gods to ease his pain,
We stood admiring his so godlike death.
His temples throbbed with stroke and throe of vein,
His eye stood fixed, his regal lips did quaver
Like aging leaves at autumn's first fierce blast;
Or, like scared soldiers in a first assault,—
And fitly, too, whose master save that hour
Knew illness never. But when I perceived
Behind me where the slaves stood all a-weeping,
Ill-omened beat of breast and hair shook horrid
From head, terror crept to my trembling foot
And crawled snake-like, increasing length and upward
Behind me, traveled on, and when it reached
My brain, it stung me hot, it maddened me;
I heard Melanios cry "How dark it grows!"
And, trying eyes, I felt myself drop earthward
Like some struck bird. How long I lay were idle

To estimate; but I awoke to strains
Of sudden music with an echoed beauty,
Which flattered with "Hail, King Eurupulos!"
While yon before me on his wonted couch,
Melanios outstretched lay white and dead.

CHOROS

Strange sorrow, bearing balm in spite of tears!

EURUPULOS

What balm, O friends, if greater grief be here?

CHOROS

What grief, Eurupulos, obeying gods?

EURUPULOS

Obedience is good, but who may know
The pleasure of the distant-dwelling gods?

CHOROS

Not far they dwell, inspiring present fears
And constant apprehension in men's deeds.

EURUPULOS

My sister, mate with me, our mother's child,
To die so rudely!

CHOROS

Think thou whom to save.

EURUPULOS

What consolation to support a brother?

CHOROS

What! thou a king and speak these vulgar words?
Better thou ne'er knewst sovereignty on earth
Than live so far from heaven thus hard to brook
A private loss when one death means a kingdom
Preserved and hailing thee successive king!
Take spirit of the gods, tranquillity,
Immunity from aches and moans of men;
Live the large life becoming kingly sway;
Bind not thy youthful soul subservient
To cares; hold high thy crown's authority;
Keep thou thy rescued love, whom, though a slave,
Ennobled in thy choice, may Zeus increase
With largess of strong heirs and happy days,
That when thou, grey, shalt hand thy scepter on,
Pure Kaludon may rise to thee one wide
And vivid blessing, sound, imperishable.
But, soft! not far a nearing footstep draws
More near.

Enter ATTENDANT

Am I not changed in spirit, voice,
Gait, all that goes before throughout my years
I passed me? Whom address I? For, methinks,
A man made god, or god made mortal first
Should hear my story lest the burden top
In marvel the less marvel of such change.

EURUPULOS

I bid thee speak: a king attends this frenzy.

ATTENDANT

Thou biddest with the smooth command of right.

CHOROS

And rightly so: for know, who ruled one hour
Ago, is dead,—Melanios.

ATTENDANT

Behold
My coldness! Naught can move me now except
Some never dreamed and never acted wonder.

EURUPULOS

And yet thou stayest when, aware of worst,
We list thy petty tale of tragedy:
The victim's blood is spilled and Koresos
In shame at muted beauty, hides. Not so?

ATTENDANT

Hides verily, for where his being keeps
Zeus knows.

CHOROS

I glean with empty hand.

EURUPULOS

Aye, Zeus:
For Zeus can penetrate the blindest flesh
And scare the lurking shame!

ATTENDANT

His body holds
No shame if benefit to Kaludon
Be other.

EURUPULOS

Practise caution, youth, feed not
The willing ire of dread and dauntless kings
That touch, therein devouring their affects,
Since sorrow oft devises tragic issues.

ATTENDANT

Thou canst not brave me, high Eurupulos,
I am a messenger from holier haunt
Than ever royal throne hath graced.

EURUPULOS

Thou slave!
Deal with me openly or die this hour!

ATTENDANT

I mean not ill to whisper entrance thus
Into thine unsuspecting and else startled
Ears, yet, so please thy will, call Koresos.

CHOROS

I fail to gather his intent.

EURUPULOS

He tempts
Me with his trickery of tongue.

ATTENDANT

Call, priest,—
He will be deaf to thy command, great king !
Aye, wert thou nearer than a king,—his friend,
Entreaty were alike most impotent.
Nor that in obstinate adherence fixed
Upon his god, he willed a deafened ear,
But that he nevermore may hear thy voice,
Since cold, kissing the temple's cold, he lies
Before Kallirrhoe !

EURUPULOS

Conduct us further :
Some mystery half-scented goads conceit.

ATTENDANT

O king and fellow-priests of Dionusos,
The gods have chosen a weak tongue in me
To publish you my legend, for I press
My fingers, weakening more and more to hide
This world, and as I look again, doubt more.
Hence unrelieved, I know not whither best
I go for counsel in my pain save that
If here to you I may release it free,
It may, in sharing, lose some poignancy
As oft as memory shall entertain
Its visitant surprise until I die.
For, as into the sacred place she hurried
Afire with wrath she kindled by her hate,
A certain pallor spelled the images,

All saving Dionusos who grew flushed
And turned ambiguous black and purpled o'er
As grapes in sunlight just at harvest-time.
In midst of weirdest portents of the gods,
The advent of moved Koresos amazed
Us more; for though the white of swoon o'ercast
His countenance, we had not so awaited
The ghostly stare and tremble of his hands.
He seemed some child in shame confessing fault,
And not a priest of god at sacrifice:—
Solemnly slow with force deliberate
Touching the fillet for the only time
And thence denouncing from this air the victim.
Nay, there he stood; a moment faced her, dumb;
Convulsively he stole the knife I offered,
Bade her uncover bosom to the blow.
Himation and tunic loosed, descended,
And hung from the confining zone.   Thereat
Or punishment from heaven or frenzy swift
At finding her so beauteous, thrilled his spirit;
Else, O ye gods, pronounce why then he rushed
To her and with one wild, despairing cry,
"Kallirrhoe!" plunging his dagger, drunk
To hilt within his own breast, fell a heap
With stream of dying kisses marking aye
Departing life, prone at her kirtle's edge.
At this distraught, a cloud bedimmed mine eyes;
I heard the smothered lamentations beat
Mine ears; I woke; I gained the door; one glance
Behind I threw, and lo! where lay the maiden

Kissing with love's dew those so long parched lips
As if to win them answer and their bloom.

EURUPULOS

Now all the gods so prosper me as now
In gratefulness of heart I honor them!

CHOROS

Speak no ill-omened word.   The gods are skilled
To blight his reign who taunteth chance untoward!

EURUPULOS

I need not counsel. . . . Thee, I mean, aye, thee
Who barest message suiting royal ear,
Command my bounty.   Yet, assure me well,—
Why tarries thus my sister o'er a corse
Erst hated, now so pitied,—woman's way?
Go thou to her.   Instant attendance here
Tell her the king demands, so shall she learn
A double joy to lodge, dead Koresos
And King Eurupulos.   What! not returned?
(Exit ATTENDANT.)

CHOROS

Strophe

Woe, woe! for a master departed I weep!
O Kaludon, surely this fate
Is beyond thee to bear and esteem,
A calamitous loss, if I seem
To measure his height to the state!

Woe, woe! I will hide me and deep
  In my grief I shall waste quite away,
  Not a tear will I spare night or day.

Antistrophe

In veriest prophecy, seeing, I cry:
  No good shall descend on a king
    Who at hate is cheered and is crowned
    With no circlet of bay but hath bound
On his brow double death that shall sting,
Envenom, and drive to insidious vanity,
  Till the jealous gods visit with scourge
  And its pitiless beat of red surge.
      (*Enter KALLIRRHOE slowly.*)

EURUPULOS

(*To CHOROS:*)

Ye might affright me, if I recked your omens.
I hear, yet scorn them as I scorned your lord,
Bending me as occasion hinted prudence!

(*To KALLIRRHOE:*)

See where she moves restored! Kallirrhoe,
Dear sister, hail! happy on whom the curse,
So strangely lighted, is more strangely lifted,
That thou mayst live to choose thee peace and rest,
Adored a princess peerless through the realm.
What! hast thou naught for me?

CHOROS

She raises lid
And gazes with no wonted pride and fire.

EURUPULOS

Ah, have they whispered how Melanios
Is dead and I—nay, pardon that I cause
Thy tears; methinks I, too, at hearing this,
Slighted no whit my heart.   Weep for the king
And then rejoice in him whom death exalts,
E'en me, thy brother, sister! me, thy brother! . .
How now—no word?   Art dumb?   Is't possible
That I, thy brother, kin and close to thee,
That I, thy king, thy lord, before all eyes
Speak and receive no answer?   Art thou mad?
Perchance dead Koresos—

KALLIRRHOE

Not that name, brother,
I charge thee, but in all the earth what else
May please thee, utter.

EURUPULOS

What distraction here?
I know what thou art overdelicate
To make prohibited mine ears: "Not strange
He took his life so long due heaven!"

KALLIRRHOE

Brother!
What word hath leaped untimely here to birth?

EURUPULOS

Hast thou not ere this, sister, wished him ill,
And for his ruin summoned every god
Thy heart knew and thy tongue could name?

KALLIRRHOE

How true
And wise thy words, O brother!

EURUPULOS

Wherein wise
And true but erst unworthy one reply?

KALLIRRHOE

There was a god, Eurupulos, whose name
To me familiar by once hated tongue
Was yet essential stranger.

EURUPULOS

Whose, I pray?

KALLIRRHOE

Him had I prayed and called in curse on life,
The priest could not have more effectual
Fallen beneath the blow than now he fell,
Turning the moment's boon to lifelong bane.

CHOROS

Dark words as ever veil her darker thought.

KALLIRRHOE

Know'st not the god who late instructed thee
The eloquence of beauty and desire,
Lilt of Aglaia's name, to call her fair?

EURUPULOS

Sister! remind me not in mockery!
Link not my love with thine ill-omened hate!

KALLIRRHOE

I mock not now, Eurupulos, I am
Not as I was, but in his death I know
He loved me and I live to die for him.

EURUPULOS

What frenzy insupportable transports
Thy senses, sister?   Art thou credulous
In folly that he died to save thy life?
Away! enrage me not!   Believe not so.
How?   Hath thy woman's heart so soon conceded
Superb esteem of him and touch of greatness
Where late thou foundest but a low intent?
List to me, sister!   Grieve for him no more.
Impute not virtue ever lived in him
Whenas he lies in death, deserving so
Compassion.   Such, no other, is the weakness
The dead ask.   Die for thee!   Recount his crime;
Think on his deeds; intriguing for this throne;
Intriguing for thy body, as thou oft

Hast owned to me in secrecy; and picture—
Not difficult—the plague from heaven he called;
Behold the incense of their putrid pyres
Arising as to him in godhead raised
Thereby, through the compliance of his god.
Thinkst thou no sleepless nights were his as out
He gazed and saw his pestilential power?
Thinkst thou he constant smiled thereat complacent
And never imaged ruin haunted him?
Thinkst thou that when he raised his eyes this morn,
No joy was his at death of thee who thus
Marked pluming of his will?   And then when he
Beheld thee standing beauteous before
The knife, thinkst thou thy loveliness restrained
Him, mercy melted at the pitch delight?
Nay! there were sudden voices in his ears
And all the dead, unburied save by heap
On heap of their staled usefulness, aye, all
Appeared that moment, raving by compact,
That when he seemed triumphant most, then least
Might power be his to strike aught but himself.
They came with bodies hungry for the earth;
These masks of murder palsied further boast,
Forbade more immolation, leered, and swore
To throttle with a million ready fingers
Invisibly that human lie and curse!

CHOROS

O King Eurupulos, if this be false,
The gods will merciless abide the deed!

KALLIRRHOE

Brother, thou shalt this once and nevermore
Again behold my face.   I shall be brief.
I know that Koresos was pure as light
The gold morn pours with lavish artlessness
Above the earth.   I knew not ere yon moment
The meaning and the wingéd wonder men
Call love.   I thought it something soft, to nestle
Like smoothness of a bird's down 'gainst the cheek,
To charm with ever-changing strangenesses,
Hunt heart with fierce desire to thrall the other,
And ever in consummate blessedness
A feverish, suspecting jealousy
At time, friends, joy, or grief unshared and known.
It is not so, and I am rapt beyond
Mere words, a part in realms I ne'er descried—

CHOROS

Look to the king, attendants, where he sways!

KALLIRRHOE

Sustained there, bathed in gentler, alien air,
All else, ennobled from the inmost heart
Of being and transmuted from the sense
And movement of my daily ease to issue
More rare from calm to higher calm, as eagles
Must mount, or men might were their oceans piled
Enmassed one on the other, calmest highest,
And in the sailless craft of contemplation

Ride quite supreme, the wide eyes lustered wider!
Aye, as among us mortal men, devising
In lands or residence vicissitudes,
Until so settled is our latest state
And blotted out the past one, that we fail
To image how all stood before the change,
So in my soul, late residence of hate —

CHOROS

Kallirrhoe! Thy brother! Look on him!

KALLIRRHOE

The sum of former days is as a dream
No sooner dreamed than dead, despite the strength
Of its phantasmal truth. And thus my life
Moves on in melody and beat of love.
And I believe he waits beyond the bourn
And stays his hands (assailing not the gods
With his impatience) from too eager reach
To me. Oh what a thought! oh what a god
To treasure soul in poise, to bring me balm
Amid severest service! If not true,—
Ah, Zeus be praised, I have been happy once!

CHOROS

Kallirrhoe! Thy brother! Look on him!
Seest not how he hath heard but half thy dreaming?
Art thou so frantic? Hast no pious tears?

KALLIRRHOE

The gods have judged: and happy are the dead
Who die unspotted deaths after such lives.
Attendants, follow.   Bear the bodies hence.

(*Exit KALLIRRHOE followed by ATTEND-
ANTS bearing the bodies of EURUPULOS and
KORESOS.*)

CHOROS

Strange is death:
Equally here they lie,
Prince and priest,
Less than living, one with buried, least.
Ah, not so: for they go,
That, so gloried here, with black-stained brow;
This, uncrowned in life, love-hallowed now!
Muteness, a song, sob, sigh,—
Such is breath.

THE END.